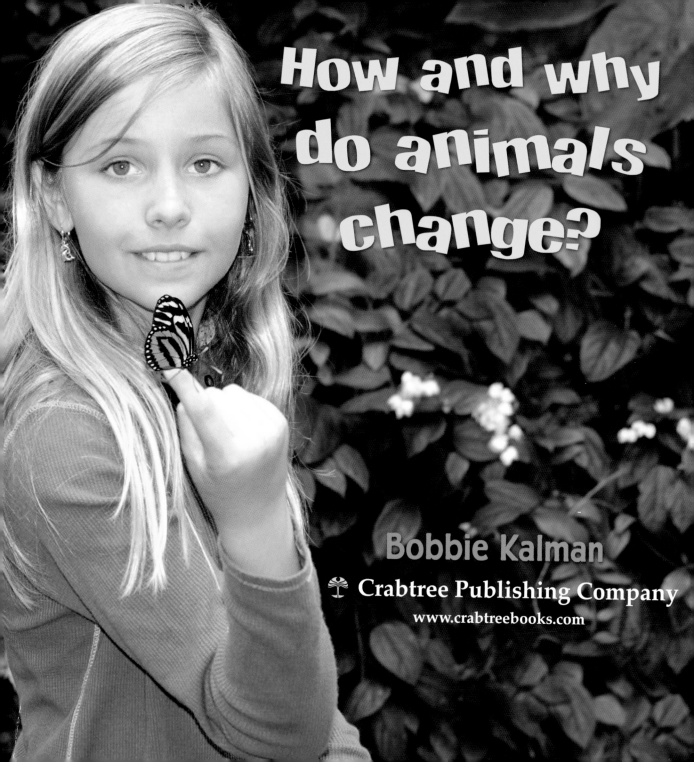

How and why do animals change?

Bobbie Kalman

🌴 **Crabtree Publishing Company**
www.crabtreebooks.com

Dedicated by Bobbie Kalman
For Damian Berti,
who loves to have fun
and makes his family very happy

Author and editor-in-chief
Bobbie Kalman

Publishing plan research and development
Reagan Miller

Editor
Kathy Middleton

Proofreader
Crystal Sikkens

Design
Bobbie Kalman
Katherine Berti
Samantha Crabtree (cover)

Photo research
Bobbie Kalman

Print and production coordinator
Katherine Berti

Illustrations
Antoinette "Cookie" Bortolon: page 18
Margaret Amy Salter: page 19

Photographs
iStockphoto: page 20
Thinkstock: page 11 (bottom right)
All other images by Shutterstock

Library and Archives Canada Cataloguing in Publication

Kalman, Bobbie, author
    How and why do animals change? / Bobbie Kalman.

(All about animals close-up)
Includes index.
Issued in print and electronic formats.
ISBN 978-0-7787-0545-1 (bound).--ISBN 978-0-7787-0600-7 (pbk.).--
ISBN 978-1-4271-7593-9 (pdf).--ISBN 978-1-4271-7588-5 (html)

    1. Growth--Juvenile literature. 2. Adaptation (Biology)--Juvenile
literature. 3. Animal life cycles--Juvenile literature. I. Title.

QH511.K35 2014   j571.8'1   C2014-903909-3
                                          C2014-903910-7

Library of Congress Cataloging-in-Publication Data

Kalman, Bobbie.
    How and why do animals change? / Bobbie Kalman.
        pages cm. -- (All about animals close-up)
    Includes index.
    ISBN 978-0-7787-0545-1 (reinforced library binding) -- ISBN 978-0-7787-0600-7
    (pbk.) -- ISBN 9781427175939 (electronic pdf) -- ISBN 978-1-4271-7588-5
    (electronic html)
    1. Growth--Juvenile literature. 2. Developmental biology--Juvenile literature.
    3. Animals--Juvenile literature. I. Title.

    QH511.K29 2014
    571.8'1--dc23
                                    2014022880

Crabtree Publishing Company

www.crabtreebooks.com   1-800-387-7650

Printed in the U.S.A./092014/JA20140811

Published in Canada
Crabtree Publishing
616 Welland Ave.
St. Catharines, Ontario
L2M 5V6

Published in the United States
Crabtree Publishing
PMB 59051
350 Fifth Avenue, 59th Floor
New York, New York 10118

Published in the United Kingdom
Crabtree Publishing
Maritime House
Basin Road North, Hove
BN41 1WR

Published in Australia
Crabtree Publishing
3 Charles Street
Coburg North
VIC 3058

Contents

How do animals change?

gills

(above) A young newt lives in water and breathes air through **gills** on the outside of its body.

(below) As an adult, the newt lives on land and breathes with **lungs**, which are inside its body.

Some baby animals look like their parents. As they grow, they change colors or shed their coats or skin to grow new ones. The bodies of other baby animals, such as frogs and butterflies, start out looking very different from their parents. Their bodies change a lot before they become adults.

Making changes

As animals grow from babies to adults, their bodies can change in other ways, too. Some animals are able to change to protect themselves. Their actions warn others to stay away.

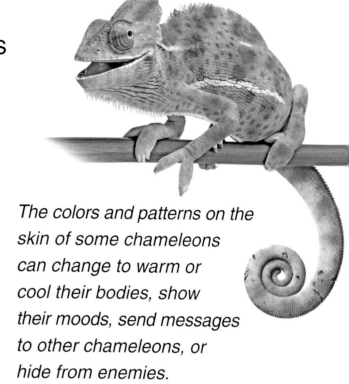

The colors and patterns on the skin of some chameleons can change to warm or cool their bodies, show their moods, send messages to other chameleons, or hide from enemies.

quills

Porcupines display their quills, or needles, when they sense danger. The quills come out when touched.

What do you think?

Which two animals change to protect themselves? How do they do it? How does the breathing of newts change?

5

Life cycle changes

A life cycle is a series of changes that begin when an animal is **born** or **hatches** from an egg. As the animal grows, its body changes in different ways until it becomes an adult. The animal also eats different foods as it grows. An adult animal can make babies of its own.

Rats are mammals. Mammals have hair or fur. Mammal mothers nurse, or feed their babies milk from their bodies.

Mammal life cycles

Mammal babies are born. Their mothers feed and take care of them until they can look after themselves.

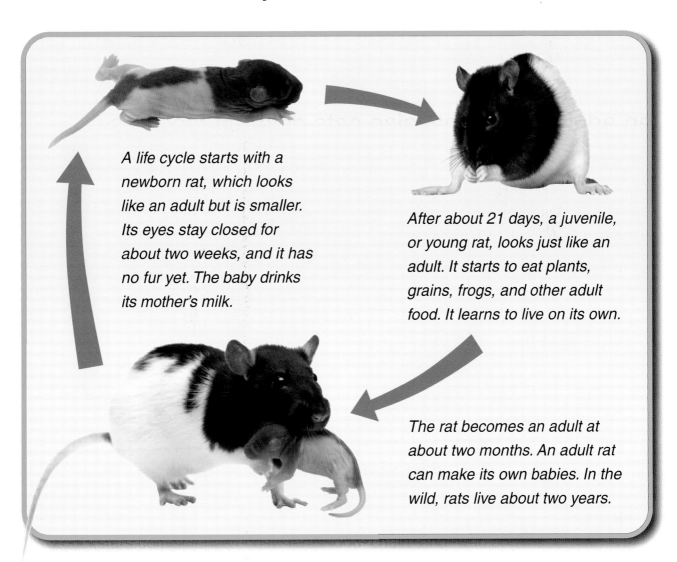

A life cycle starts with a newborn rat, which looks like an adult but is smaller. Its eyes stay closed for about two weeks, and it has no fur yet. The baby drinks its mother's milk.

After about 21 days, a juvenile, or young rat, looks just like an adult. It starts to eat plants, grains, frogs, and other adult food. It learns to live on its own.

The rat becomes an adult at about two months. An adult rat can make its own babies. In the wild, rats live about two years.

Reptile changes

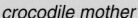
crocodile mother

Snakes, lizards, turtles, and crocodiles are reptiles. Reptiles start their life cycles inside eggs. After they hatch, they grow and change. Most reptile mothers do not look after their babies, but alligator and crocodile mothers stay nearby to protect them.

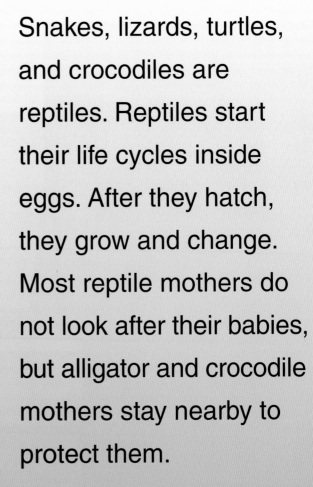

These baby crocodiles will start to take care of themselves about two weeks after hatching.

Growing new skin

Baby reptiles look like their parents, but they are much smaller. Their bodies are covered with thin bony plates called scales. Scales protect a reptile's body, but they do not grow as the body grows. As new skin grows underneath, reptiles must shed their old scales. Called molting, most reptiles shed their scales in small pieces.

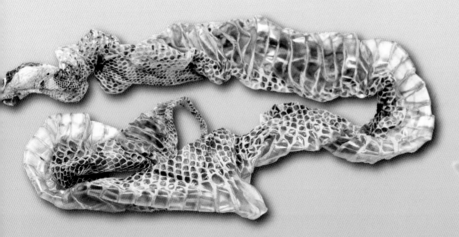

(above) Snakes shed their skin in one long piece. This skin belonged to a rattlesnake.

(right) This baby lizard is a chameleon. Chameleons shed their scales about once a month until they stop growing. They eat their old skin.

From down to feathers

Birds also hatch from eggs. As babies, they are covered in a soft, fluffy coat called down. They stay in their nests and cannot fly until they grow feathers. The babies then molt, or shed, their fuzzy down.

A covering of down keeps these great egret chicks, or baby birds, very warm.

red-footed
booby chick

red feet

This red-footed
booby chick will soon
lose its down, grow feathers, and be
ready to fly. Its beak will turn blue and
its feet red, like those of its parents.

11

Winter changes

Some animals live in places with very cold winters, such as the Arctic. The Arctic is at the northern part of Earth. Arctic fox kits, or babies, are born in the summer with gray fur. As adults, their gray fur is replaced with white fur in winter, which then grows gray again in summer.

Short ears, extra body fat, and furry paws all help the fox keep warm. Arctic fox kits look like their parents and are fully grown by the time they are a year old.

what do you think?

How does having white fur help arctic foxes sneak up on their prey? Prey are the animals that predators such as arctic foxes hunt and eat.

Learning life skills

As animals grow and change, they learn new skills, such as climbing, flying, swimming, and hunting. These skills help them find food and protect themselves from predators, or animals that hunt and eat other animals. The mothers of some baby animals teach them the skills they need to survive, or stay alive.

Baby bears learn to climb trees to stay safe, find nuts to eat, and to sleep.

Most birds learn to fly once they grow feathers.

This squirrel is eating a cactus fruit in the desert. It learned to get most of the water it needs from its food.

Predators like these lions must learn to hunt. This mother lion has taken her cubs hunting.

What do you think?

What skills do some animals learn that you also learn? What skills would you like to learn as you grow older that animals cannot learn?

15

Dragonfly changes

Some animals go through stages, or big sets of changes, as they grow into adults. They change their body shapes and parts. This set of changes is called **metamorphosis**.

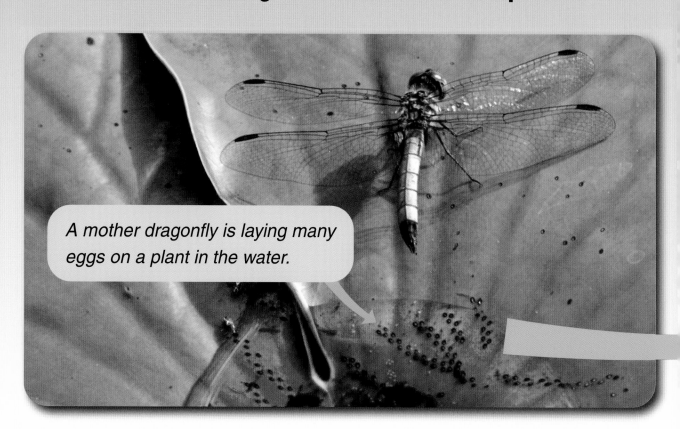

A mother dragonfly is laying many eggs on a plant in the water.

Incomplete metamorphosis

A life cycle with three stages is called **incomplete metamorphosis**. The three stages in the life cycle of a dragonfly are egg, nymph, and adult.

A nymph hatches from each egg. Nymphs look a bit like adults but have no wings. They live and find food in the water. Nymphs molt many times as they grow.

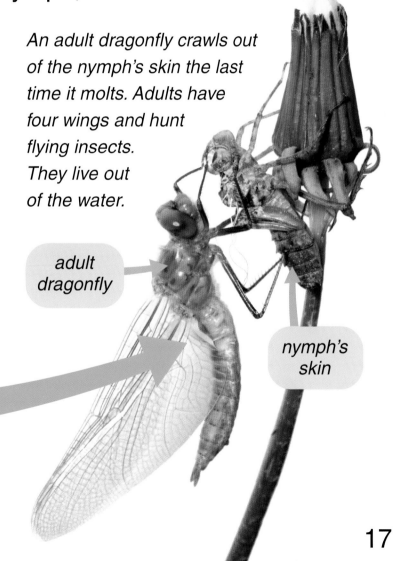

An adult dragonfly crawls out of the nymph's skin the last time it molts. Adults have four wings and hunt flying insects. They live out of the water.

adult dragonfly

nymph's skin

From egg to butterfly

Animals that go through **complete metamorphosis** change completely. Insects such as butterflies go through complete metamorphosis. They have four stages in their life cycles: egg, larva, pupa, and adult. The insects look very different at each stage.

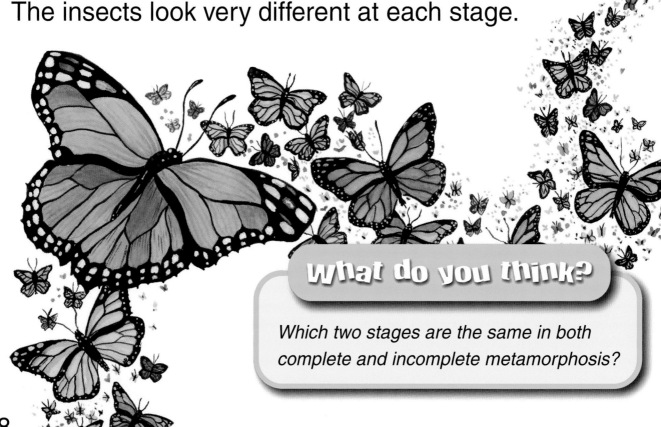

What do you think?

Which two stages are the same in both complete and incomplete metamorphosis?

Butterflies start their lives inside eggs laid by adults.

The adult butterfly emerges from, or comes out of, the chrysalis. It has wings and six legs. Adult female butterflies can lay eggs.

A larva, known as a caterpillar, hatches from each egg. It has a long body with many legs, but it has no wings.

The caterpillar builds a hard case, called a chrysalis, around itself. It becomes a pupa inside and stays there until it becomes an adult.

The caterpillar eats the leaves of plants and grows quickly. Then it is ready for the next stage.

19

Frog changes

Frogs also go through complete metamorphosis. They start their lives inside eggs called spawn. Tadpoles hatch from the eggs. They look completely different from frogs. Different body parts grow as the animals change from tadpoles to adults.

spawn

tadpole

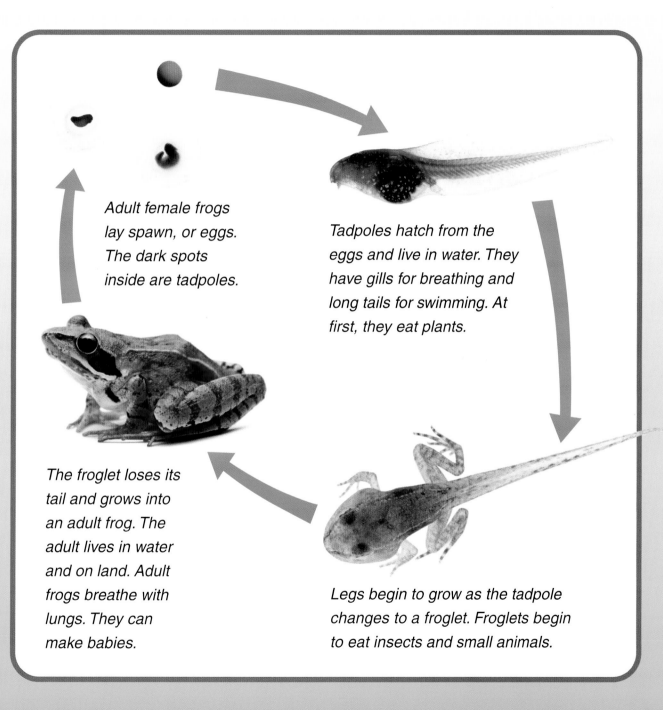

Adult female frogs lay spawn, or eggs. The dark spots inside are tadpoles.

Tadpoles hatch from the eggs and live in water. They have gills for breathing and long tails for swimming. At first, they eat plants.

The froglet loses its tail and grows into an adult frog. The adult lives in water and on land. Adult frogs breathe with lungs. They can make babies.

Legs begin to grow as the tadpole changes to a froglet. Froglets begin to eat insects and small animals.

21

Do you know?

(A)

(B)

Find the animals on
this page that match
the animals in the
questions below.

(C)

(D)

(E)

1. Which animal changes
   color in winter?

2. Which animal sheds
   its skin as it grows?

3. Which two animals go
   through metamorphosis?

4. Which animal grows
   feathers?

5. Which four animals
   hatch from eggs?

Answers

1. D arctic fox
2. E chameleon
3. A frog,
   B butterfly
4. C bird
5. A, B, C, E

Learning more

Books

Kalman, Bobbie. *Animals grow and change* (Introducing living things) Crabtree Publishing Company, 2008.

Kalman, Bobbie. *Caterpillars to Butterflies* (It's fun to learn about baby animals). Crabtree Publishing Company, 2009.

Kalman, Bobbie. *How do animals change?* (My World). Crabtree Publishing Company, 2011.

Kalman, Bobbie. *Metamorphosis: Changing Bodies* (Nature's Changes). Crabtree Publishing Company, 2005.

Kalman, Bobbie. *Tadpoles to Frogs* (It's fun to learn about baby animals). Crabtree Publishing Company, 2009.

Slade, Suzanne. *What Do You Know About Life Cycles?* (20 Questions Science). PowerKids Press, 2008.

Suen, Anastasia. *A Lion Grows up* (Wild Animals). Capstone Publishing, 2005.

Websites

Kids Discover: Spotlight: Metamorphosis
www.kidsdiscover.com/spotlight/metamorphosis-kids/

San Diego Zoo Kids: Mammal: Arctic Fox
http://kids.sandiegozoo.org/animals/mammals/arctic-fox

Words to know

born (bawrn) adjective Describing the time when a baby animal emerges, or comes out, live from its mother's body

gills (gils) noun Body parts found in animals for breathing air under water

hatch (hach) verb To break out of an egg

lungs (luhngs) noun Organs used by animals to breathe oxygen from air

metamorphosis (met-uh-MAWR-fuh-sis) noun The big sets of changes in body shapes and parts that some animals go through as they become adults: (**complete metamorphosis** has four sets of changes; **incomplete metamorphosis** has three sets of changes)

A noun is a person, place, or thing.
A verb is an action word that tells you what someone or something does.
An adjective is a word that tells you what something is like.

Index

For Every
Individual...

The
INDIANAPOLIS PUBLIC
Library

Renew by Phone
269-5222

Renew on the Web
www.indypl.org

For General Library Information
please call 275-4100